Two Snakes

Retold by Edel Wignell
Illustrated by Marjory Gardner

sundance
A Haights Cross Communications Company

One day two snakes went out to look for food.

The first snake saw an egg.
"Yum!" he said.
"An egg for my lunch!"

3

The second snake
saw the egg, too.

"Yum!" he said.
"An egg for my lunch!"

5

"It's my egg!"
said the first snake.

"It's my egg!"
said the second snake.

They were both hungry,
and they both wanted the egg.

7

"It's mine!" said the first snake.

"It's mine!" said the second snake.

The two snakes slid
around and around the egg.

"It's mine! It's mine!" they hissed.

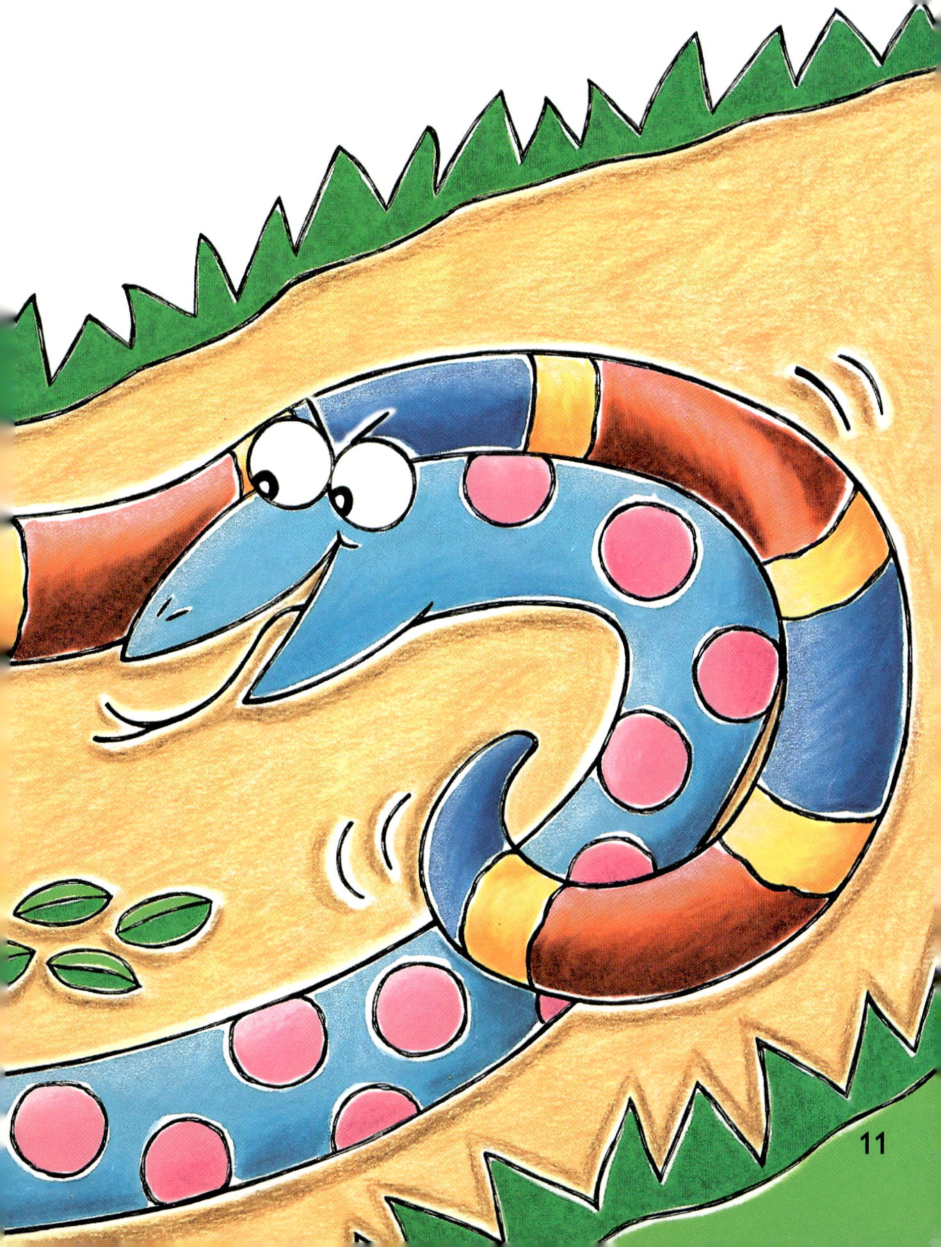

The first snake grabbed
the second snake's tail.

The second snake grabbed
the first snake's tail.

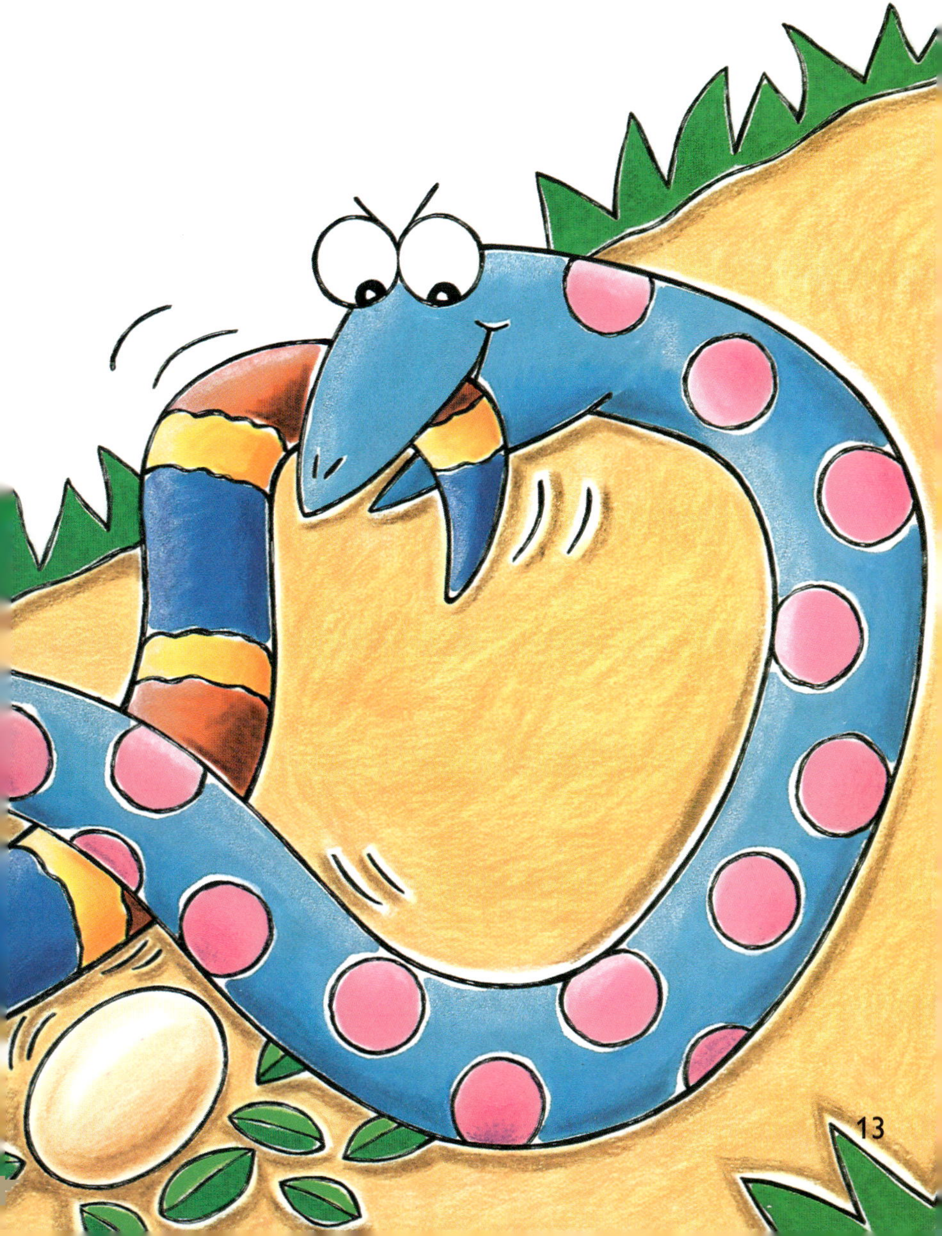

The first snake bit the second snake.

The second snake bit the first snake.

They bit and bit and bit
and slid down the hill
until all that was left was . . .

15

an egg!